Earth's Changing Rivers

by Neil Morris

Raintree

Chicago, Illinois

Printed and bound in China by South China Printing Company
07 06 05 04 03
10 9 8 7 6 5 4 3 2 1

Editorial: Keith Ulrich
Design: Erica Barraca
Picture Services: Michelle Lisseter and Bridge Creative Ltd
Illustrations: Bridge Creative Services Ltd
Production: Sal D'Amico

Cover photograph of power boat speeding down winding waterway reproduced with permission of Getty Images/Stone.

The publishers would like to thank
Margaret Mackintosh for her assistance
in the preparation of this book.

Every effort has been made to contact copyright holders of any material reproduced in this book. Any omissions will be rectified in subsequent printings if notice is given to the publishers.

Library of Congress Cataloging-in-Publication Data

Morris, Neil, 1946-
  Earth's changing rivers / Neil Morris.
    p. cm. -- (Landscapes and people)
  Summary: Looks at the geography and people that make up river regions throughout the world, focusing on the changing characteristics of both.
  Includes bibliographical references (p.   ) and index.
  ISBN 1-4109-0175-0 (hc) 1-4109-0346-x (pb)
  1. Rivers--Juvenile literature. 2. Landscape changes--Juvenile literature. 3. Stream ecology--Juvenile literature. 4. Nature--Effect of human beings on--Juvenile literature. [1. Rivers. 2. Landscape changes. 3. Stream ecology. 4. Ecology. 5. Nature--Effect of human
beings on.] I. Title. II. Series: Morris, Neil, 1946- Landscapes and people.
  GB1203.8.M66 2003
  551.48'3--dc21

                2003002184

Acknowledgments
The publishers would like to thank the following for permission to reproduce photographs:
p. 5 Alamy Images; p. 15 Mark Carwardine/Bruce Coleman; p. 8 Gary Braasch/Corbis, p. 16 Galen Rowell/Corbis, p. 18 Nick Wheeler/Corbis, p. 20 Brian A. Vikander/Corbis, p. 22 Patrick Ward/Corbis, p. 23 Michael S. Yamashita/Corbis p. 25 Lester Lefkowitz/Corbis, p. 26 Lloyd Cluff/Corbis, p. 27 Liu Liqun/Corbis, p. 29 James Marshall/Corbis; p. 13, 24 Stone/Getty Images; p. 6 John W. Warden/Natural Science Photos, p. 10 C Dani- I Jeske- Milano/Natural Science Photos, p. 17 Ken Cole/Natural Science Photos; p. 14 Dave Watts/Nature Picture Library; p. 21 Phil Cooke; p. 12 Robert Harding Picture Library.

Contents

Any words appearing in the text in bold, **like this,** are explained in the Glossary.

What Is a River?

What do you think of when you think of a river? Is it a torrent of white water carrying a bobbing canoe fast downstream? Or is it a gently flowing ribbon of water winding between trees and fields? Whichever one you think of, you're right. A river can be both of these things, and many others, too.

A river is any large amount of **freshwater,** usually flowing to a sea or ocean. Most rivers start on high ground and flow downhill in their own channels.

Water flows in small streams before these become deep and wide enough to be called a river. Some rivers flow for many miles before they reach the sea. Sometimes they flow into another river or a **lake.** A lake is a body of water surrounded by land.

This world map shows where the world's ten longest rivers are. The longest of all, the Nile River, flows for 4,144 miles (6,670 kilometers) from central Africa all the way north to the Mediterranean Sea.

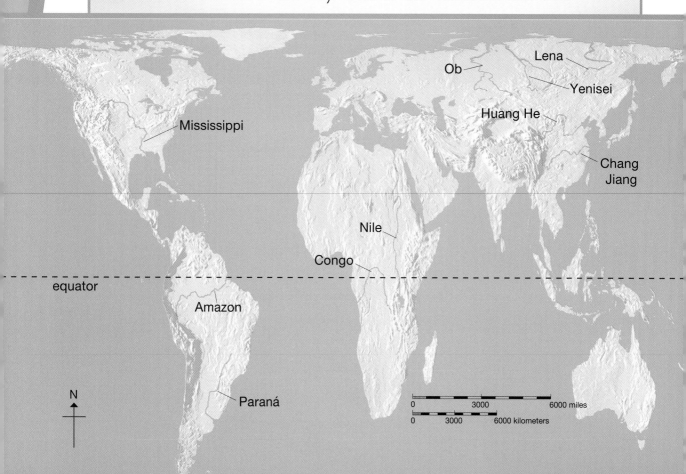

Rivers change a lot on their way from high ground to the sea. They also change the land through which they flow. The way in which people use rivers changes them, too.

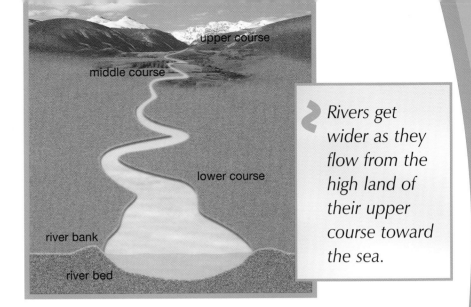

upper course
middle course
lower course
river bank
river bed

Rivers get wider as they flow from the high land of their upper course toward the sea.

World of rivers

There are rivers flowing across the land on all the world's continents except very cold Antarctica, where the water is frozen. In this book we look at how rivers form and how they shape the **landscape** through which they flow. Each river is different and flows through a different landscape. They make **valleys, gorges,** and waterfalls, and sometimes flow over their banks and flood the nearby land.

People used rivers in the past and still use them today. Rivers are important to humans for many reasons, including drinking water and transportation, but in recent times we have tried to change them so that they are even more useful. This has brought benefits, but it has also brought problems.

Many of the world's rivers are very busy. They flow through towns and cities. This is the Huangpu River in Shanghai, China.

How Do Rivers Form?

When rain falls on land, some of it seeps into the ground and some stays on the surface. The water that stays on the surface forms tiny streams. Many of the tiny streams join each other as they rush downhill. As more streams join together, the water flow becomes larger. When the flow of water is wide, we call it a river. The beginning of a river is called its **source.**

> *The waters of the Merced River rush downhill over waterfalls and **rapids** in Yosemite National Park, California.*

Headwaters

Water always flows downhill, and so rivers flow from high ground to the sea. Streams near the river's source form its **headwaters,** where the water is still shallow. It flows quickly, tumbling down steep slopes. The streams run together to make a small river. As the river flows, it wears away the land on either side and starts to cut its own **channel** into the ground.

The region that includes a river's source and headwaters is called its upper course. Here the water usually flows fast and wildly, because the land is steep and often rocky.

The water cycle and the river basin

The sun heats water on land and in the world's oceans (as shown below). The heat changes water into water vapor. This happens everywhere—in seas, ponds, and even in small puddles. The vapor rises into the air, where it cools to form droplets of water. These droplets join together to make clouds, and eventually the water falls back to earth as rain or snow. The water runs into the river from the higher ground around it. This is called the **river basin.** The highest ground, which separates one river basin from another, is called the watershed. The river takes the water back to the ocean, where the cycle starts all over again.

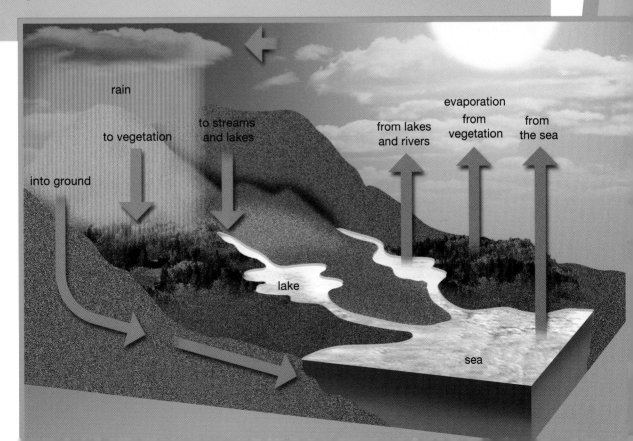

Middle course

Farther downhill, in the middle course, smaller rivers often join the main river flow. The smaller rivers, which are like branches of the big river, are called **tributaries.** They swell the flow of the river, making its **channel** wider. Most big, wide rivers have many tributaries.

Lower course

When the river reaches flatter land, it flows more calmly and becomes wider. Then it often starts to wind and loop around. Curved bends form in the river, called **meanders.** The flatter land of the lower course allows the river to easily overflow its banks. This happens after heavy rainfall or when snow melts quickly near the **source** of the river, which brings more water into the river from the **river basin.** The flat area beside the river that can sometimes flood is called the **flood plain.**

> The Pearl River makes such a large meander at this point in Mississippi that it almost turns back on itself.

At the mouth

The river ends at its **mouth.** This is the place where the river's water flows into the sea. Most rivers are at their widest near their mouth. The wide part of a large river near its mouth is often called an **estuary.** Here the river's **freshwater** mixes with the salty water of the sea.

When they near the sea, many of the world's biggest rivers split into smaller channels. This is because as the flow of water slows, small stones and **silt** cannot be carried along, and the river can no longer carve a single channel. The fan-shaped area through which the channels flow near the mouth of a river is called a **delta.** The name comes from the shape of a Greek letter that looks like a triangle (Δ = delta).

The Missouri River is the main tributary of the Mississippi, the longest river in North America. The two rivers join near the city of St Louis. They both have many other tributaries. The Mississippi fans out and flows through a delta into the Gulf of Mexico. Because of its shape, this is called a bird's-foot delta.

From the source of the Missouri in the Rocky Mountains to the Mississippi delta, this "great river" (which is what Mississippi means) is more than 3,728 miles (6,000 kilometers) long.

Changing Landscapes

As a river flows, the force of its moving water washes away loose soil and pieces of rock. In this way the river cuts its own **channel** in the ground. Its rushing water then carries along large **boulders** and smaller stones, as well as tiny pieces of rock. This moving load scrapes against the bottom and sides of the river's channel, making it deeper and wider. The process of wearing away rocks and carrying pieces away is called **erosion.**

Carving a gorge

Erosion helps rivers carve out **valleys.** Over a long period of time, some make steep valleys called **gorges,** or **canyons.** The Grand Canyon in Arizona is the largest gorge in the world. In places it plunges to a depth of around 5,900 feet (1,800 meters). At its widest point, it is 18 miles (29 kilometers) across. The Grand Canyon was carved over millions of years by the Colorado River, which flows through it. As the river wore away the rocks, movements deep underground lifted the surrounding land upward. Every year, summer heat, winter frost, and rain make cracks in the canyon's rocks wider.

Gravel, sand, and clay

Boulders and stones bump into each other as the river carries them along. As the river begins to slow in its middle course, pieces break off and heavier rocks drop to the bottom. The smaller pieces rub and scrape against the land as they are carried along. These smaller stones form gravel, which is carried farther **downstream.** The gravel breaks down into smaller fragments of sand and clay. As the river flows more slowly, it deposits (drops) these fragments as **silt.** Some silt is carried all the way to the sea.

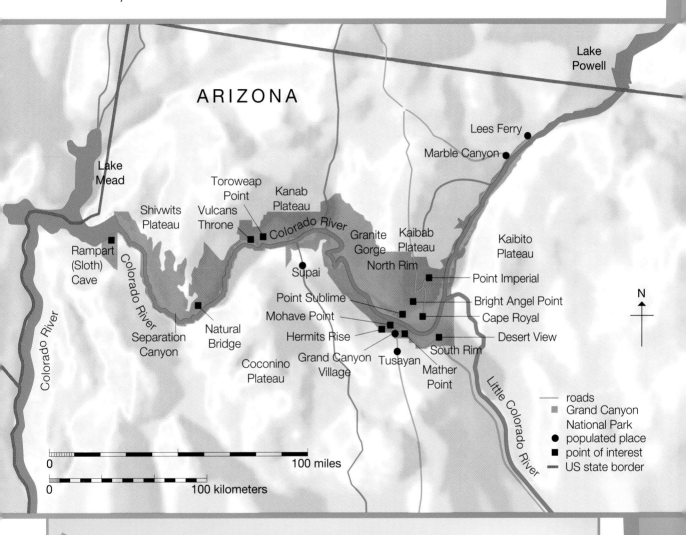

*The shaded area shows the **national park** around the Grand Canyon. The Colorado River flows from the top right of the map, on its way from the Rocky Mountains to the Gulf of California. There are many points of interest where visitors can look down into the canyon. These are areas of harder rock that have not been eroded by the river. The river cuts a winding path through areas of softer rock.*

Waterfalls

When a river drops suddenly from a higher to a lower level, it forms a waterfall. Most waterfalls are found in the upper course of a river, where the water flows through mountains. Waterfalls form when a river crosses from hard rock, which is hard to break down, to softer rock, which wears away more easily and becomes a step. The harder rock becomes a **cliff,** and the river flows over this to make a waterfall.

Flooding

Rivers flow evenly throughout the year if rainfall provides them with a constant supply of water. When there is much more rain than usual, however, a river can rise above its normal level. Then water pours over the riverbanks and causes a flood.

*Every year there are floods in Bangladesh. This is because much of the country is a **flood plain** for two great rivers—the Ganges and the Brahmaputra—and their **tributaries.** Very high rainfall at certain times of the year causes the rivers to flood, which is often made worse by tropical storms.*

Drying up

When there is little or no rainfall for several months at a time, rivers may dry up. This happens a lot in dry regions of the world, leaving dry, cracked riverbeds. Dry riverbeds in deserts are called wadis. Because the river **channel** is already carved, it fills up again quickly when there is heavy rainfall.

The Horseshoe Falls, on the Niagara River, is about 2,200 ft (670 m) wide and is separated by an island from the American Falls. Together they make up Niagara Falls.

Niagara Falls

Halfway between Lake Erie and Lake Ontario, on the border between the United States and Canada, the Niagara River plunges over the edge of a high cliff. This makes the famous Niagara Falls, the name of which means "thunder water." The falls are as high as 190 feet (59 meters) at their highest point, from the top of a cliff formed out of a hard kind of limestone rock called dolomite. The water plunges onto softer sandstone and shale rock below. As the softer rocks are worn away at the bottom of the cliff, the swirling water weakens the cliff and pieces of limestone break off. Because of this, the Falls are slowly moving back toward Lake Erie—at a rate of about 3 feet (1 meter) a year.

Changing Life

Water is needed by all forms of life—plants, animals, and humans. That is why rivers are important to all life on Earth. Many plants grow beside rivers, where they are well watered. They provide food for animals that live near the river or that come to the river to drink. The same is true for humans, who also catch the river animals, including fish, for food.

In the upper course of a river, the water is usually cold and flows fast. Few plants can survive in these conditions, so there is very little for animals to feed on. The small amount of vegetation that does grow is enough to provide food for young insects like mayflies. A few snails and leeches may also find enough to eat in the river's upper course.

Along the river bank

Farther down the river, as it becomes calmer and wider, more plants grow along the banks and in the river itself. These provide food for insects and other animals, which are eaten in turn by frogs and fish. Fish are able to swim against the **current** in this part of the river. Their presence attracts larger animals, like otters, that make resting places and nests in the river bank. The living things in and around the river depend on each other for food and survival.

The most unusual thing about the Australian platypus is its long, flattened snout, often called a duckbill. It uses this to feed on the river bottom, diving for up to a minute and sliding its bill along the bed to catch worms, shellfish, and insects.

Feeding on the river bed

Some animals have become specially adapted to life beside and in the river. One of these is the platypus, an egg-laying **mammal** that lives only in Australia. Its toes are joined together by skin, giving it webbed feet that help with swimming. The platypus also has claws, which are useful for digging its burrow in the river bank.

Near the mouth

Many water birds like to live near the mouths of rivers. There the water generally moves slow, and the birds can keep an eye open for fish and other small animals swimming out to sea.

In the great rivers

Most dolphins live in the ocean, but some have adapted to great rivers—including the Amazon of Brazil, the Yangtze of China (also called the Chang Jiang, see map page 4), and the Ganges of India. There are different species, or kinds, of dolphin but they have many things in common. They all have long, slender beaks and poor eyesight. This river dolphin lives in the Yangtze, and feeds on fish and shrimp.

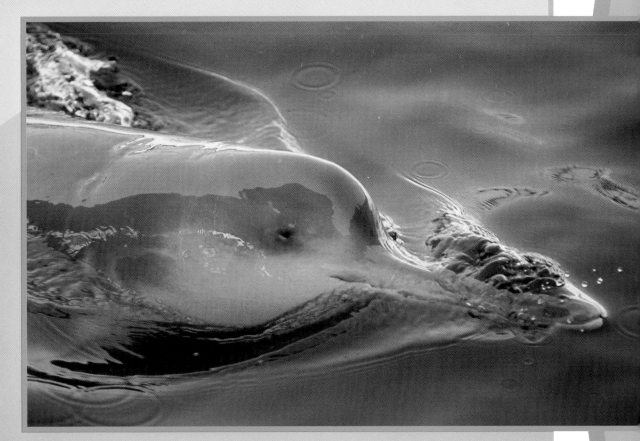

Fish

There are fish in most of the world's rivers. They feed on many smaller river creatures and in turn provide food for larger animals. Some **freshwater** fish, such as grayling and brown trout, like the clear water of fast-moving rivers. Others, such as catfish and carp, prefer the calmer, muddy water of the lower course. The presence of fish was one reason why people chose to settle near rivers, but in recent years fish populations have been greatly harmed by **pollution.** Pollution not only harms fish, it also kills the food they eat to survive.

Swimming upstream

Salmon are used to all kinds of water conditions because they swim the length of rivers. A salmon's life begins in the gravel at the bottom of a stream. When a young fish hatches out of its egg, it swims all the way down the river to the sea. Some salmon stay in the sea for up to five years. Then they return to exactly the same river and begin the difficult journey back to where they started life. This journey can take several months, and the fish may swim thousands of miles. Scientists believe that salmon recognize their home river by its smell. It is difficult swimming **upstream** against the **current,** and they have to leap over **rapids** and even waterfalls (right). Once they have reached home, female salmon lay their eggs. Pacific salmon then die, but Atlantic salmon may return to the sea to begin the cycle once again.

Water birds

Many different kinds of birds live near rivers, feeding on fish and other water creatures. Most kingfishers nest in holes in banks, often in the middle course of a river. They perch on a branch hanging near or over the water, ready to dive when they see a passing fish. Herons feed in a different way. They prefer to wait at the edge of the river, on the bank, or wading in shallow water. They often stand very still, and then suddenly dart their head down to grab their **prey.** Ducks spend a great deal of time swimming on the water. Some dive to feed, while others feed on the surface, eating small animals and weeds.

*This great white egret belongs to the heron family. Egrets often make their nests in reed beds near the **mouths** of rivers, where they find plenty of food— fish, insects, and plants.*

Changing Settlements

Rivers have always been important to people. Early humans followed the course of rivers as they moved around, hunting wild animals and gathering roots and berries for food as they went. Rivers provided water and offered plenty of food to catch.

Ancient civilizations

Many thousands of years ago, groups of wandering hunters decided to settle near rivers and grow their own food. Small riverside **settlements** grew into villages, and some became important towns and cities. The water and mud of the rivers, called sediment, made the surrounding land rich, **fertile,** and good for farming. By about 7000 years ago farming villages were developing around rivers in many parts of the world. **Civilizations** grew along the rivers with their own languages, religions, and ways of life.

As settlements and civilizations grew up alongside rivers, they often became the setting for important ceremonies or celebrations. This ceremonial barge is on the Irrawaddy River in Myanmar (Burma).

Between the rivers

One of the earliest civilizations developed in a region of Southwest Asia called Mesopotamia, which means "between the rivers." Two great rivers, the Euphrates and the Tigris, flowed through this region, which is part of present-day Iraq. The rivers begin in the highlands of modern Turkey and flow south, joining to form one river before reaching the Persian Gulf. The area around and especially between the two rivers was good farming land. Reeds that grew in the rivers and surrounding **marshes** were useful for building boats and houses.

The earliest cities in the south of Mesopotamia, such as Ur and Uruk, were part of an empire called Sumer. Later this became Babylonia, with its magnificent capital and the legendary Hanging Gardens of Babylon. The Gardens (one of the Seven Wonders of the Ancient World) were built on terraces fed by water from the Euphrates. The land in the north, around the Tigris, became known as Assyria.

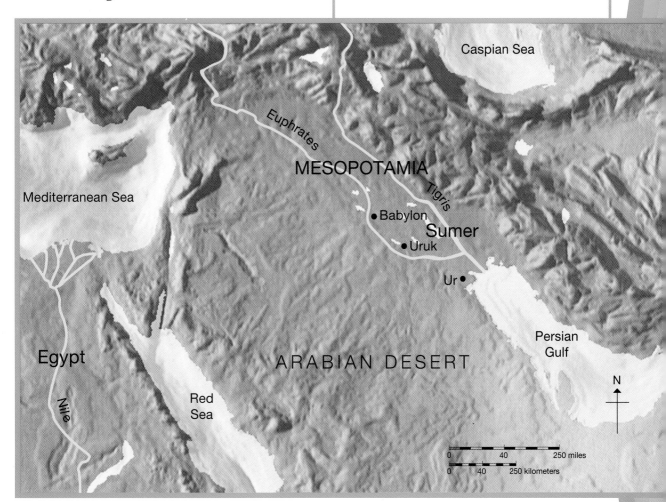

Caspian Sea

Euphrates

MESOPOTAMIA

Tigris

Mediterranean Sea

• Babylon

Sumer

• Uruk

Ur •

Egypt

ARABIAN DESERT

Persian Gulf

N

Nile

Red Sea

| 0 | 40 | 250 miles |
| 0 | 40 | 250 kilometers |

Long and Yellow Rivers

Ancient Chinese **civilization** also grew up around two great rivers, and they are both still important today. The Huang He (or Yellow River) was named after its muddy yellow color. This comes from the fine mud and clay carried by the river. This is deposited to make the surrounding land especially **fertile** and good for farming. Further south, the Yangtze River (or Chang Jiang) is used for river transportation (see page 23) and for making electricity (see page 26). It has been called China's main road, and it leads to the largest city and busiest port in China—Shanghai. The city lies near the **mouth** of the Yangtze.

Living on stilts

Long ago people realized that rivers often flood their banks. This led them to start building houses on stilts. This meant they could live as close as possible to the river, where the land is most fertile, without their homes being flooded. Stilt houses are still popular for the same reason today. Many of the people of Thailand in Southeast Asia live beside the Chao Phraya and Mae Khlong rivers. Their stilt houses are made of bamboo, **palm leaves,** and straw.

These Thai families live in modern wooden stilt houses.

Xingu National Park

Many indigenous groups settled along the Amazon River and lived beside its **tributaries** in the Amazonian **rain forest.** In 1961 a large area around the River Xingu was made into a **national park** to protect this traditional way of life. Traditionally, men go out each day in canoes, using spears and nets to catch fish. The women are experts at making pots from the clay they collect on the riverbanks.

The Gift of the Nile

The ancient Egyptian civilization grew up beside the longest river in the world—the Nile. The ancient people who settled on its banks used the Nile's water for drinking, bathing, and watering their fields of wheat and barley. Devices called shadoofs (shown in the picture) were used to raise the water out of the river. They also built reed boats and used the river as the easiest way of getting around. Today, most Egyptians still live along the fertile strip of land beside the Nile, and great cities such as Cairo have grown up along its banks. **Tourism** is an important **industry** to modern Egypt, and many foreign visitors choose to see this ancient country from boats that act as floating hotels.

River transportation

Through the ages rivers have been used for carrying both goods (things for selling) and people. They were always especially useful for traders, providing a fast link between trading centers before there were good roads or any trains. As people explored new lands, they traveled along rivers and built towns and cities beside them. Today, roads and railroads allow people to move goods more quickly than they could by river, but rivers are still used for transportation, particularly in areas difficult to reach by road.

 This barge is making its way along the Rhine River in Germany.

Barges

Waterways are still important for transporting big, heavy loads. Barges are used to carry goods along rivers from factories to large seaports. There the goods are transferred to ships, which then carry them all around the world. Barges are used on the Rhine River, which begins in the Swiss Alps and flows through Germany and the Netherlands to the North Sea. It is Western Europe's main waterway, passing through the **industrial** cities of Germany to the major Dutch port of Rotterdam. In 1992 a **canal** was opened to link the Rhine with the Danube River, allowing barges to travel all the way from the North Sea to the Black Sea.

Ferries

Riverboats are still used as passenger ferries. In China large four-decker boats travel down the Yangtze River. They take five days to carry people from the city of Chongqing to the port of Shanghai. Ferries are useful in cities, too. In Paris boats on the Seine River offer a good way for sightseers to get around. In Tokyo, the capital of Japan, locals and tourists can travel in a comfortable "river bus" up the Sumida River. The river bus sits low in the water, so it does not hit the many bridges over the river. Many people feel that using rivers more often for transportation could help to solve traffic problems in some of our cities.

Changing Rivers

Many different kinds of **industries** have traditionally been based beside the world's rivers, and they still are today. This began because fast-flowing rivers could be used to turn waterwheels and run mills and other machinery. When steam engines replaced watermills, rivers remained just as important, because steam is produced by heating water.

Power stations

Although electric machines have replaced steam engines, water is still needed to produce the electricity. A great deal of the world's electricity is produced in power stations that burn fuel to boil water, creating steam. The steam turns **turbines** that make electricity. **Nuclear** plants also produce steam to turn turbines. In all these processes, water is also needed to cool machinery, so a location near a river is very useful.

Many different industries choose to build their factories or mills next to rivers to take advantage of the water supply. This riverside paper mill is in British Columbia, Canada.

Factories and farms

Some factories and farms change rivers by taking too much of their water to cool machines or water fields. Others change them in an even more unfortunate way, by **polluting** them with waste and chemicals. It is easy to get rid of waste by pouring it into a river, but this can have terrible effects. **Industrial waste** can poison fish, kill plants that other animals eat, and ruin rivers. Farmers using weedkillers and **pesticides** can also harm rivers if these chemicals drain into rivers from the soil.

Drinking water

Many people in poorer parts of the world do not have proper supplies of clean water. Yet in richer regions, people are using far more water today than they ever have. The Colorado River, for example (see page 10), is controlled by eleven major **dams** and used to supply water to seven states and a small part of Mexico. More than 25 million people drink water from the river, so that its delta is now a dry mudflat. Hardly any water reaches the sea, because it is all taken along the way.

*To make it safe to drink, river water is cleaned at a treatment plant. It passes through filters made of sand and gravel. Then chemicals are added to make sure that the water is free from any harmful **bacteria**. Harmful bacteria can cause diseases.*

Water power

People build **dams** across rivers so that they can use the power of rushing water to make electricity. The dam creates a **reservoir,** or storage area, and water is allowed to drop down through a special pipe. There the water turns the blades of a **turbine** that drives a generator. This generator produces electricity. Controlling rivers in this way brings problems as well as benefits.

Controlling the Nile

The annual Nile flood was essential to the **civilization** of ancient Egypt because the Egyptians needed **fertile** land to farm, but modern Egyptians needed more control over the river's waters. After ten years of construction, the Aswan High Dam was opened in 1971. During the rainy season, the dam holds back the Nile's rising waters. This creates a huge reservoir more than 310 miles (500 kilometers) long.

The Aswan High Dam is made of earth and granite. It took ten years to build and is over 2.2 miles (3.6 km) wide, 364 feet (111 m) high, and 131 feet (40 m) thick at the top.

Benefits and problems

Water stored in the reservoir is used to irrigate (water) farmland during dry periods. This means that more crops can be grown. The dam is also used to produce electricity. Changing the river's flow has caused problems, too. The dam stops fertile mud from moving **downstream.** Farmers have to use more chemicals to fertilize their land instead of the river's deposits of **silt,** or sediment.

> While the massive Three Gorges Dam is being built, the waters of the Yangtze have been diverted around it.

Three Gorges Dam

The world's biggest dam, the Three Gorges Dam, is being built on the Yangtze River in China. This huge project, started in 1993, will be completed in 2009. The concrete dam will be 607 feet (185 meters) high and 1.3 miles (2.1 kilometers) wide. Its 26 turbines will generate more power than any other dam's.

Flood control

More than a million people will have to move because of the huge **lake** that will be created behind the Three Gorges Dam, which will make the water level rise to 574 feet (175 meters). Planners say that 15 million people downstream will be better off because they will be protected from floods. This is important because the Yangtze River floods regularly and has killed more than 300,000 people in the last 100 years.

Into the future

The world's rivers are constantly changing. This is not surprising when you think that just a slight change in the pattern of rainfall can have an effect on even the biggest rivers. If a river changes its course or floods or dries up, the people who live nearby can be seriously affected. That's why people try to control rivers, but rivers are always changing, which is why they are so fascinating.

River Facts and Figures

The world's longest rivers
Measured from the source of the farthest tributary to the mouth of the main river.

river	continent	length in miles	length in km
Nile	Africa	4,145	6,670
Amazon	South America	4,007	6,448
Chang Jiang	Asia	3,915	6,300
Mississippi	North America	3,741	6,020
Yenisei	Asia	3,442	5,540
Huang He	Asia	3,395	5,464
Ob	Asia	3,361	5,409
Paraná	South America	3,032	4,880
Congo	Africa	2,920	4,700
Lena	Asia	2,734	4,400

Largest river basins
The basin is the area drained by a river and its tributaries.

river	continent	area in sq miles	area in sq km
Amazon	South America	2,722,000	7,050,000
Paraná	South America	1,600,400	4,145,000
Congo	Africa	1,312,700	3,400,000
Nile	Africa	1,293,400	3,350,000
Mississippi	North America	1,244,800	3,224,000
Ob	Asia	1,149,800	2,978,000
Yenisei	Asia	996,100	2,580,000
Lena	Asia	961,400	2,490,000
Amur	Asia	786,900	2,038,000
Chang Jiang	Asia	756,800	1,960,000

Highest dams

dam	river, country	height in ft/m
Rogun	Vakhsh, Tajikistan	1,100 / 335
Nurek	Vakhsh, Tajikistan	984 / 300
Grand Dixence	Dixence, Switzerland	935 / 285
Inguri	Inguri, Georgia	892 / 272
Vaiont	Vaiont, Italy	859 / 262
Chicoasén	Grijalva, Mexico	856 / 261
Tehri	Bhagirathi, India	856 / 261
Kambaratinsk	Naryn, Kyrgyzstan	836 / 255
Kishau	Tons, India	830 / 253
Mauvoisin	Drance de Bagnes, Switzerland	820 / 250
Sayano	Yenisei, Russia	803 / 245
Mica	Columbia, Canada	800 / 244
Guavio	Guavio, Colombia	797 / 243
Ertan	Yalong, China	787 / 240

At Angel Falls in Venezuela, water plunges from the top of fairly flat sandstone. This is the world's highest waterfall.

Highest waterfalls

waterfall	river, country	height in ft/m
Angel	Churun, Venezuela	3,211 / 979
Tugela	Tugela, South Africa	3,106 / 947
Utigard	Jostedal, Norway	2,624 / 800
Mongefossen	Monge, Norway	2,539 / 774
Yosemite	Yosemite Creek, U.S.	2,424 / 739
Ostro Mardola Foss	Mardals, Norway	2,152 / 656
Tyssestrengane	Tysso, Norway	2,119 / 646
Cuquenán	Arabopó, Venezuela	2,001 / 610
Sutherland	Arthur, New Zealand	1,902 / 580
Kjellfossen	Naero, Norway	1,840 / 561

Worst floods

location	year	estimated deaths
Huang He, China	1931	3,700,000
Henan, China	1887	900,000
Bangladesh	1970	400,000
China	1642	300,000
Henan, China	1939	200,000
Chang Jiang, China	1911	100,000
Bengal, India	1942	40,000
Bangladesh	1965	30,000
Japan	1786	30,000
Bangladesh	1963	22,000

Glossary

bacteria tiny living things that can only be seen through a microscope and that can sometimes cause illness

boulder large stone that has been worn smooth

canal human-made waterway

canyon deep, steep-sided valley, usually with a river flowing at the bottom of it

channel deep groove carved by a river

civilization advanced culture, or a people with an advanced culture

cliff steep rock face

current strong, steady flow of water in one direction

dam large barrier across a river that holds back water

delta fan-shaped area at the mouth of some rivers, where the river splits into many smaller channels

downstream in the direction of a river's flow, toward its mouth

erosion wearing away parts of the earth's surface, especially rocks

estuary wide part of a river near its mouth, where the river's fresh water mixes with the salty sea water

fertile having rich soil and producing good crops

flood plain flat area on either side of a river that is under water when the river floods

freshwater water that is not salty

gorge steep-sided valley, often with a river flowing through it

headwaters streams flowing from the source of a river

industrial waste poisonous materials or chemicals given off as part of the process of an industry, like a factory

industry business, often factories making something

lake body of water surrounded by land

landscape natural scenery

mammal warm-blooded animal, the female of which feeds its young with milk. Dogs, cats, whales, bats, and humans are all mammals.

marsh boggy wetland

meander tight curve or bend in a river

mouth end of a river, where it flows into the sea

national park area where animals, plants, and land are protected

nuclear to do with a form of power or energy released by the splitting of atoms

palm leaves leaf of a palm, a tropical tree with no branches

pesticide chemical used to destroy insects or other pests that are harmful to plants

pollution damage from harmful substances

prey animal that is hunted and eaten by another animal

rain forest thick forest found in warm tropical areas with heavy rainfall

rapids part of a river where the water moves very fast over rocks

reservoir human-made lake where water is collected and stored

river basin area drained by a river and its tributaries

settlement place where people live permanently

silt fine layer of mud and clay

source place where a river begins

tourism business of organizing vacations and visits to places of interest

tributary small river that flows into a larger one

turbine machine with blades that are turned by moving water

upstream against the flow of a river, toward its source

valley low area between mountains

Further Reading

Beatty, Richard. *Biomes Atlases: Rivers and Lakes*. Chicago: Raintree, 2003.

Chambers, Catherine. *Mapping Earthforms: Rivers*. Chicago: Heinemann Library, 2001.

Oxlade, Chris. *Earth Files: Rivers and Lakes*. Chicago: Heinemann Library, 2003.

Telford, Carol, and Rod Theodorou. *Amazing Journeys: Down a River*. Chicago: Heinemann Library, 1998.

Index